Napoleon Wasn't Exiled

A WINE AND TRAVEL JOURNAL BY VICTOR RALLO JR.

ABOVE: Napoleon, by Gregg Hinklicky.

PREFACE

Most of the time when I taste wine, I am in the midst of utter confusion, not a great venue to appreciate wine. I rarely open the bottle with the care intended because I am rushing through my busy life. How the hell can you truly experience the beauty, elegance, and complexity in a great wine when you're totally stressed out? As soon as I leave the hustle and bustle of daily life, my blood pressure drops, my phone stops ringing (or rings a lot less) and I really start to relax. This is when I like to taste, drink, and evaluate wine; this is when my senses seem to be the freshest.

Join me as I sit back, relax, and drink some great Italian wine on my *giro* through Tuscany.

TABLE OF CONTENTS

Foreword 4

Day 0 7

Day 1 9

Day 2 17

Day 3 27

Day 4 29

Day 5 33

Day 6 35

Day 7 45

Day 8 53

Day 9 56

Day 10 62

Day 11 67

Day 12 80

Day 14 89

Special Thanks To: 96

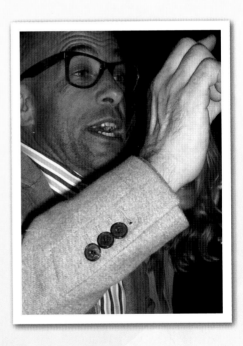

FOREWORD

Whenever I think of Victor Rallo, Jr., my mind wanders to the Roman poet Ovid. Both Vic and Ovid started out as lawyers, wearing that profession's sober robes of respectability. Ovid tells us that when he tried to write legal briefs, poetry issued forth, causing him to realize that his calling was in the arts, not in the law. Vic, inspired by his father, whom I knew as "Big Vic," abandoned the courtroom for the kitchen. He and his brother Bobby, also a lawyer turned restaurateur, have kept the dreams and memory of their dad alive and well. In fact, they have carried them onto a higher plateau.

Ovid's masterpiece, *The Metamorphoses*, recalls all of the changes of forms that took place from the beginning of time itself to his own day, around the beginning of the Christian Era. Vic is similarly involved in the changing of forms – that is, in the art of progress. He takes local, fresh ingredients and transforms them into delicious dishes. A recipe is a metamorphosis, as is the process of fermentation, which changes grapes to wine.

Victor Rallo will tell you that I am his wine mentor. Actually, I was his wine mentor. Today, Vic is as capable as any restaurateur in evaluating the merits of wines, from the international to the domestic, and from the exalted to the everyday. Vic knows the full story of the vine, including its most treasured secrets. He does not need me, except for friendship and a few laughs.

The new adventure for Vic is to be an author. His expertise and passion shine through in his intrepid Tuscan travelogue. To him and his family, let me say, *"Salute!"*

Anthony J. Verdoni
October 2011

DAY 0

WHEN WE TRAVEL OVERSEAS, EVERYONE IN THE FAMILY BRINGS a backpack and a carry-on bag with wheels. Two years ago in Rome, the airline lost one of our bags. This cost us two days, as I had to drive back to Rome, Fiumicino Airport on two consecutive days to finally retrieve the lost bag. After that episode, I changed the rules and now enforce a carry-on only baggage policy. This guarantees that your luggage arrives with you, but checking in at the airport and going through security is still a nightmare!

Belts off, shoes off, laptops out of the bags. Then it happens, everyone's

ABOVE: Merlot grape cluster, Bolgheri.

OPPOSITE: San Domenico church in Siena, Italy.

BELOW: The Tuscan Countryside.

worst nightmare: "Sir, can you please open your luggage?" Underwear flying everywhere; embarrassing, like a yard sale at Newark International Airport. Having your luggage with you has its benefits, but sometimes I question if it's really worth it because it makes getting through security an Olympic event. Gameboys and headphones, laptops and cell phones, and of course, I have to go to the bathroom right in the middle of the security and passport check line. Hurry I can't wait! I'm afraid that I may go in my pants!!! Good news! We made it.

SUNDAY AUGUST 14, 2011

DAY 1

Enoteca Osticcio
Via Matteotti 23
Montalcino, Tuscany

Complexity wears many dresses, and fills many parts of our lives. Navigating Newark International Airport and the plane ride overseas with my wife Kari and three children Eli-13, Jake-11, and Jack-11 is complex and tiring. We just landed in Rome and I am trying to relax.

The next scene is easy; we drive the car from Rome to the ancient, historic town of Montalcino. That is, after getting through the car rental process in Rome: *Auto Noleggio* (car rental). Five stories up but only four down, here we go round and round. I hate Italian multi-level parking garages. It always seems like a Houdini act to get where you really want to be. We finally plug in the GPS and away we go, with Sarah Palin aboard. That's what we call the woman speaking on the GPS. My children named the voice Sarah Palin and it stuck, so Sarah Palin

she is. We are on the road now and things are looking up. I know what is in store when we arrive in Montalcino: great food and fine wine.

Wine can sometimes be simple, but the great wines are usually complex. Our first wine is Valentini Trebbiano d'Abruzzo 2008. It is a very rewarding start. After the overnight plane trip and a two-hour plus drive to Montalcino, a Valentini wine is a tough starting point. Someone has to do it though, and the sommelier recommends it, so why not? I say bring it on! Our journey has officially begun...

The food and service at Osticcio, a small *enoteca* in Montalcino, complement this wine and make our task easier. When the sommelier pulls the cork, I am ready to go. Valentini wines are made in the vineyards, a rare practice. The grapes are never moved or transported to the cellar. Fermentation is literally done in tanks in the fields. Valentini's process is unlike the majority of wineries in the world. Most wineries transport the grapes to the winery where sorting, crushing, destemming, and fermentation takes place. Valentini believes that the grapes begin to oxidize during the transportation and that the quality of the wine is compromised.

On the nose, the wine is full of minerals and has a musty, almost "Thrift Shop" personality. After a few minutes in the glass, a tingle of pine and citrus fruit becomes evident, and the wine comes alive with great acidity and layers of fruit. Don't mistake the bubbly effervescent spirituality of this wine as something that has gone totally astray. This is normal in open fermentation wines, especially wines made by Valentini. Valentini wines last. From a good vintage, ten years is not unusual. Avoid drinking this Trebbiano young; I recommend a few years in the bottle before opening.

Valentini wines have garnered many awards, creating tremendous demand. They are still produced in very small quantities and only in exceptional vintages. The Montepulciano d'Abruzzo from Valentini has been produced only a couple of times in the past decade. If you see a bottle on a restaurant wine list or in a good wine shop, buy it and experience the wine of a true master first hand.

As time passes, people get old, cars break down, and your children grow up. In Montalcino, I can guarantee you that as time passes, the wine only gets better. My colleague, "The Wine Professor" Anthony Verdoni, calls Brunello di Montalcino "Time in a Bottle."

WINE #2

COL D' ORCIA BRUNELLO DI MONTALCINO

1995

One of the most difficult wine making job in Italy is making wine from a single varietal under the strict scrutiny of the "DOCG," the highest level of classification for wines in Italy. Brunello di Montalcino is one of those wines; 100% Sangiovese Grosso made under the watchful eyes of the DOCG regulations. Does anyone remember the 2003 Brunello scandal? BRUNELLOGATE!

In 2008, upon release of the 2003 vintage of Brunello di Montalcino, the Italian Government began an investigation into producers who were suspected of adding international varietals such as Cabernet Sauvignon, Merlot, and Petit Verdot into Brunello di Montalcino. That practice is strictly prohibited by DOCG regulations because Sangiovese is the only grape permitted in the production of Brunello di Montalcino. Traditionally, the hue of Brunello wines and Sangiovese is a translucent, almost red brick color. Many producers in Montalcino were mysteriously achieving a purple, deep ruby color associated with certain international varieties, but not with Sangiovese-based Brunello di Montalcino. Today, the investigation continues and my job is not to decide who is cheating. My job is to judge great wines, so I judge the wine that is in the bottle and let the DOCG Committee worry about the rest.

Col d'Orcia is a very traditional, large Montalcino producer, consistently producing high quality wines. So, why not try a 1995 Col d'Orcia Brunello di Montalcino after the Valentini Trebbiano? After all, this is our first day in Italy. Musty, like an old leather bound book, but still carrying the muscular tannins of a younger Brunello – quite amazing after sixteen years. Will those tannins eventually round out and bring balance and har-

mony to this wine? I'm not sure. I think I should tell the sommelier to hold a bottle for me, so I can come back next year and try it again.

The simple, yet delicious pastas and great service at Enoteca Osticcio do just fine for us. The jet lag is now far behind and we are in full swing. So we walk through the heart of Montalcino to the Hotel Dei Capitani that will be our home base for the first five days of the trip. Hotel Dei Capitani is a quaint hotel, but is by no means five star. It has a pool and a great continental break-fast, which are both big plusses. This is always my home in Montalcino. If you're looking for me here, go straight to Hotel Dei Capitani.

The kids are dying to go for a swim, so Eli, Jake, Jack, and I invade the Hotel Dei Capitani pool. The pool is small, but is the only one in town, so this is the spot. Honeymooners, Germans, English, and Frenchmen beware: we are going to make big splashes after the great food and wine. Everyone gets wet, including the Gucci-clad prima donna on her reserved chaise lounge.

ABOVE: The only pool in Montalcino.

OPPOSITE: Summer flowers, Montalcino.

15

DAY 2

I HAVE ALWAYS BELIEVED THAT THE SOUTHERN SECTOR OF THE Montalcino zone produces the most aromatic, elegant Brunellos. Today that belief is solidified. The hillside vineyards just below the Abbazia Sant' Antimo, one of the most beautiful and well preserved Abbeys in Italy, provide the perfect exposure for the wines of Uccelliera. Maybe Andrea and Paola—the husband and wife team at Uccelliera—have the luck of the lord on their side, but one thing is evident: Uccelliera is becoming a top-tier Brunello producer.

Today, I preview the amazing 2010 vintage from the cask and some vintages of Uccelliera wines in the bottle during lunch at Andrea and Paola's home with my family.

OPPOSITE: Secret vineyards of Uccelliera.

Again, Brunello di Montalcino is governed by the strict DOCG guidelines. The wine MUST be made from 100% Sangiovese, aged for a minimum of two years in wood and four months in the bottle prior to release. It is available for sale in January of the fifth year after the harvest. We are currently drinking the five star ***** 2006 vintage.

Andrea's wines are unique because he produces super-elegant Brunellos with layers of complexity by manipulating the oak aging. What do I mean? I taste the 2010 Brunello from barrels and casks, and not from just one cask but from several different wood casks of varying sizes (250, 500, 1,500 hectoliter barrels), from a variety of French forests (Nevers, Allier, Troncais), and from large oak casks made in the Veneto from Slovenian oak. Each of the oak barrels receives a different treatment to the wood. The cooper (barrel maker) toasts the wood to the winemaker's standards (i.e. neutral, medium, or dark toast).

So in my explanation of the tasting, I taste samples of the 2010 Brunello from eight to ten different oak barrels made of different wood, different toasts, and different sizes. To evaluate the same wine as it develops many diverse intricacies and complexities from the oak is fascinating. Andrea's mastery comes to fruition when he blends or assembles these casks together to make the wine that will be bottled as Brunello 2010. Guess what? I did all of the hard work of tasting the wines, so I can give you all a preview of this wine. Don't be too anxious, though, because the wine will not be available until January 2015.

ABOVE: Andrea Cortonesi, at the window.

OPPOSITE: Abbazia di Sant'Antimo.

When I drink Andrea's wines I like to be really fresh, because this is when my senses really burst with joy. When I drink Uccelliera wines…I Feel the Earth Move Under My Feet!

Uccelliera Brunello di Montalcino
Barrel 1486 "Riserva di Vittorio"
2010
This was my favorite barrel

Well, elegant would be the best place to start, with firm but not overpowering tannins and the beautiful, crisp acidity of Sangiovese. My true appreciation lies in the complexity and structure that Andrea gets from his assemblage and aging techniques. It is here that we get the layers of cherries and even wild strawberries, entangled in the spiritual, mineral laden terroir of Sant'Antimo.

By bottling time, this wine will be ageworthy for twenty to twenty-five years. I guarantee a 97-plus rating, but only time will tell. On my recent trip to Piemonte, Michele Chiarlo, the famous Barolo producer, told me that Italy's great reds hold up for ten to fifteen years. Anything beyond fifteen years is outstanding, and I believe him! Great red wines are like great friendships, you can get more than fifteen years out of both.

WINE #4

UCCELLIERA ROSSO DI MONTALCINO

2004

WINE #5

UCCELLIERA BRUNELLO DI MONTALCINO

2001

Andrea and Paola prepare an excellent meal. The Ragu is the best I have ever tasted. We all drink red wine – Kari and the kids too. Like they say: When in Rome, do as the Romans!! Or rather, when in Tuscany, do as the Tuscans!

I am still eating and drinking well into Day 2. Everyone expects us to eat and drink with them. Who am I to say no?

Remember, Italians take pride in their food and wine, and I want to get invited back. I continually tell myself to eat and drink. It is my best insurance policy for a repeat invitation.

ABOVE: Lunch at Uccelliera.

Today was one of those WOW visits for a
wine lover like me. By fate, divine intervention
or some pure, good old-fashioned luck I end up
in "RESTA", a small locale 400 meters outside of
the Brunello DOCG and just a few kilometers
from the village of Buonconvento.

My friend Alberto is the owner of Tenuta
Oliveto, a small rising star among Brunello pro-
ducers. Alberto has a lovely girlfriend named Livia, and her family comes
with quite a story in the world of Tuscan wine.

Livia's father Claudio is the COO of Altesino winery, one of the
largest and most recognized Brunello producers. He has held that job for
nearly thirty-five years. Livia's mother, Anna Lisa, is a wine aficionado
who began giving tours around Montalcino to tourists in the early 1980's,
building great connections with all of the Brunello producers. Through
her journey, guided by her appreciation for life, wine, art, and food, she has
blossomed into one of the foremost experts in Montalcino.

Anna Lisa told me that she and her family ended up in "RESTA", an
ancient home and church (which once existed as a monastery) by some
sort of "*miracolo*." When Claudio and Anna Lisa began to really inspect

OPPOSITE: The vineyards of Fattoria Resta.

23

the home, they found scripted into the basement walls a prayer to wine from the 1500's. Why a prayer, they do not know, but Anna Lisa assured me that this constituted a sign. "RESTA" was meant to become their home and winery.

When we pull off the main road from Montalcino to the sign pointing toward "RESTA", we begin to climb through the beautiful landscape leaving the town of Montalcino in the distance. We are on our way to a very special place. When Alberto parks the car I know I am in for a treat. The vineyard is pristine, breezy, spiritual, and small - absolutely perfect. The late afternoon summer breeze whistles through the hillside, providing natural ventilation to the grapes. In every locale where great vines grow, you feel the same refreshing breeze. It is a common thread in all great vineyards.

"RESTA" translates to "rest or stay" and if invited, I would have!!!!

Anna Lisa's wine, Martin del Nero, is named in honor of the Franciscan Monk who built "RESTA", her home, in the 1500's. Martin Del Nero wine is made at Fattoria Resta a few kilometers outside of Montalcino. The vines in the 5,400 square meter vineyard are grown by Anna Lisa and winemaker Paolo Caciorgna. Anna Lisa makes only one wine from 100% Sangiovese (a Montosoli clone). The wine is aged in second and third passage oak for twelve to fourteen months, then in the bottle for at least four months prior to release. Only 4,500 bottles of Martin del Nero are produced each year and distribution is for family, friends, and a lucky few others. Anna Lisa's friends include Sting and Trudie Styler, restaurateur Danny Meyer, and Silvio Berlusconi, plus her new friend ME, who will be hounding her for wine nonstop so my friends can taste this wine too.

On Anna Lisa's card there is a quote, and in English it reads, "In Life you need four things: you need to know, you need to do, you need to know how to do...but especially, you need to let others know." I think this quote is best under-stood after drinking a bottle of her wine, Martin del Nero!! Note: I review this wine on DAY 7.

OPPOSITE: The catacombs of Resta.

DAY 3

The Palio

THE PALIO, THE ANCIENT HORSE RACE OF SIENA, SHOULD BE ON everyone's bucket list!! Archaic, historic, medieval, enchanting and another excuse to drink great wine while savoring delicious Sienese food. But this book is about Napoleon, not horses. The Palio will be the next book!

OPPOSITE: Palio head.

DAY 4

WOMEN IN WINEMAKING: WHO WOULD HAVE BELIEVED WOMEN WOULD play a prevalent role in a typically male dominated profession? As I taste wine from around the world, I have experienced many great wines made by women. I have asked many of them about the turbulence they experience taking on this traditionally masculine occupation. Women winemakers from Piemonte to Toscana to the Southern Islands have told me of their difficulties, and the oppression of thoughts, views and techniques. I can truly say that they are a thing of the past now, and that women are making wine just as well as men.

Today I met another female winemaker, Paola Gloder, of Poggio

OPPOSITE: A view of the Montalcino landscape from Hotel Dei Capitani.

Antico in Montalcino. At the vine ripe age of twenty years old, Paola received a proposition from her father: would she move to Montalcino and run the family-owned Poggio Antico Winery? As a young, aggressive and spirited woman, she thought about it for a few hours and agreed to take on the job and responsibility. The rest is history. Today, twenty-five years later, Poggio Antico is distributed in nineteen countries and is established as one of the premier Brunello producers in Montalcino.

I am fortunate to taste several of her wines with her over a delicious lunch at the restaurant on the grounds of Poggio Antico. Ristorante Poggio Antico, run by Chef Giovanni Luca Di Pirro, is destined to be the first Michelin starred restaurant in the Siena province. Please do not miss the tasting menu for lunch or dinner. The food is delicious.

WINE #7
POGGIO ANTICO BRUNELLO DI MONTALCINO
2004

ABOVE: Victor and Paola Gloder, Poggio Antico.

OPPOSITE: Giacomo Neri and Victor.

I think Paola chose 2004 because she wants me to understand how Poggio Antico ages. This Brunello is now seven years old and in my estimation still a baby, but also very drinkable. As Brunellos age, the tannins and acidity start to come into balance and the wine really begins to develop harmony in the bottle. The complexity of the wine starts to show in many different ways, with layers of fruit, leather, the terroir, and flowers.

This wine is showing all that and more. Dried cherries in the mouth with a beautiful crisp acidity, and delightful aromatics which I think is due to the altitude at which the vineyards lie. Poggio Antico has the highest vineyards in Montalcino, 1,200 meters above sea level. Poggio Antico has always been a quality producer, and continues to stand out even during tough economic times.

The 2006 vintage is rated five stars in Montalcino, but, to my surprise, the quality in Montalcino seems to be slipping. With nearly 250 producers today, the amount of Brunello being produced is one-hundred times what it was in 1980. That is a hell of a lot of wine. Couple this vast expansion in production with the current economic climate, forcing many producers to compete to sell their wine. This pushes prices down and puts quality on a back burner. Do not get me wrong, there are still great Brunello producers and producers throughout Italy who consistently create super-high quality, world-class wines. What is disturbing is that the mid-level producers throughout Italy are suffering immensely.

WINE #8
CASANOVA DI NERI "TENUTA NUOVA" BRUNELLO DI MONTALCINO
2006

To my knowledge, no winemaker in the world has had as much success as Giacomo Neri in the past ten years. He has garnered numerous awards and recognition, and in 2001 his Tenuta Nuova Brunello 1997 was rated the Top Wine in the world on Wine Spectator's, annual top 100 list. His wines transport Sangiovese to another place, another planet, the next level of elegance that places his wines among the very best in the world.

We eat a very simple delicious Tuscan dinner with our families in the tasting room of his home/winery. Despite all of his success Giacomo is still very humble, as are his wife and children. We feel like we are at home.

The 2006 Tenuta Nuova drinks to rave reviews: 100 points from James Suckling and 97 points from the Wine Spectator. By my account, those reviews are well deserved and on the mark. On the nose I immediately get some herbal notes of fresh mint, hints of graphite and minerals, surrounded by the essence of fresh cherries.

The beauty of Giacomo's wines is the elegance. They are absolutely deliciously drinkable now and amazingly ageworthy for fifteen to twenty-five years. Unlike many other winemakers, Giacomo understands harmony and the proper balance of fruit, tannins, acidity and oak. His wines remind me of the harmonies in an old Simon and Garfunkel tune. Giacomo Neri, you are a Rock, you are an Island!

I learned many things from my mentor Anthony Verdoni. Maybe the most important tip he has taught me is a simple one: never let anyone remove your wine glasses at a tasting, because it is important to continue evaluating wine throughout the tasting or meal. Always remember that longevity is ultimately determined in the glass. The Tenuta Nuova in my glass opens beautifully and deserves its 100 point score! Bravo Giacomo. I cannot wait to try the Casanova di Neri Brunello di Montalcino Cerretalto 2006 in January 2012.

DAY 5

WE LEAVE MONTALCINO AND DRIVE TO MONTEPULCIANO FOR THE DAY and night. I have never been to Montepulciano and want to survey the scene. I break one of my basic tenets of Italian travel: never, ever go somewhere for just one day. There is too much to see and do and it usually creates utter confusion. Montepulciano is beautiful, but Montepulciano will be a story for another trip, another book. SORRY! One day and night is not enough time to visit any medieval Italian village, especially Montepulciano.

DAY 6

THE MORNING OF AUGUST 19 TAKES US TO MARINA DI SCARLINO WHERE we board a sailboat for a six day tour of Isola di Elba. So, when I pick up my writing it will be right where Napoleon was let off. Napoleon was supposedly "exiled" to Elba, but you should see this place. It is definitely not Siberia! Somebody please exile me to Elba.

After speaking to my friend Giovanni Folonari, I decided to charter a boat for our trip to Isola di Elba. The Folonari family is legendary in Italian wine making history. He told me that the island is much too busy in late August, but that it is so beautiful to see by boat. This allows you to see all of the beautiful ports and lay of the island without having to deal with

ABOVE: Fortezza d'Elba.

OPPOSITE: Fishing boats, Isola di Elba.

the hustle and bustle…unless you really want to.

After some research and after many phone calls, I find Marco from www.sailingtheweb.com. Marco speaks perfect English and acts like a gentleman. He finds us a great boat, an eighteen-meter Nauti-Swan, named Alpha-Centuri. He also finds us the perfect crew in Bruno and Anna. Nauti-Swan boats have a huge deck and plenty of space below for sleeping and lounging. I now have to make the choice — sailboat or hotel? After doing a cost/benefit analysis on the sailboat versus hotel rooms and car, I choose the boat. This proves to be a memorable, unbelievably perfect

OPPOSITE: Captain and crew.

37

choice and makes the vacation one that the family will remember for our entire lives.

Swan sailboats were originally built in Holland, designed to sail in ocean races throughout the world. Today, the Nauta-Swan company is owned by the Ferragamo shoe family and is based in Florence, Italy.

Our chartered boat is preparing to sail around the world. Bruno and Anna (boyfriend and girlfriend) purchased the boat, Alpha-Centuri, about a year ago in Sardegna. They have been working on it for eleven months and doing some charters to offset the cost of restoration. When the restoration is complete, in late October, they will begin their adventure sailing around the world. When we meet Anna and Bruno, it is love at first sight. We immediately hit it off. *Vela, vela, vela.*

They say everything tastes better at sea. I hope this is true of the wines I brought on board. Tonight, I will pull the cork on the first bottle!!

The arrow points to "GREPPO."

WINE #9
BIONDI-SANTI "TENUTA GREPPO" BRUNELLO DI MONTALCINO
2004

ABOVE: Entering the famous estate of Biondi Santi.

38

Biondi-Santi is the father of Brunello di Montalcino. Ferruccio Biondi-Santi created and developed the Brunello clone of Sangiovese and vinified the first documented Brunello di Montalcino in 1888. If you are a serious wine lover, and there is someone or some producer that is so historically and integrally associated with the region, you MUST taste his or her wines. It is my duty to drink Biondi-Santi Brunello di Montalcino.

When tasting and judging wines I usually taste two bottles of the same wine to assure that I received a fair sample of the wine. I am, however, on a boat and when I arrived at the Marina in Scarlino, Bruno and Anna thought I was nuts boarding a boat with four cases of wine. There was a limit to how much wine I could stow on board, so one bottle of each wine was the protocol for this trip. Can you sink a boat with too much wine?

The cork in this bottle was in great shape, but I cannot say the same about the wine. The wine was very light in color, typical of Biondi-Santi wines. This bottle had passed its time. It was lackluster, with very little fruit. The acidity had nearly vanished and the tannins were almost gone.

Biondi-Santi Brunello di Montalcino is the one of the most expensive on the market. I usually enjoy their wines very much. Whether it was the bottle or the vintage, it did not do it for me. Normally Biondi-Santi wines are among the most ageworthy Brunello's. They typically last fifteen-fifty years. By the way, I let the wine sit for another hour and tried it again. BASTA done!

Tonight's dinner:
Osteria La Botte Gaia - Cucina & Cantina
Owner Riccardo
Porto Azzurro
Viale Europa
Isola di Elba
Phone: 0039056595607

The meal at Osteria La Bottle Gaia is great, fresh, delicious, and very typical of the region. We all eat fresh-caught island fish, Spigola with onions, tomatoes, and black olives baked in a wood fired oven. The fish is served filleted after cooking and finished with local olive oil and sea salt. Simple and perfect, I gave it a "10." I almost forgot the *primi* (first course), a five fish dish, prepared local style. Octopus with ceci beans and olive oil, prawns with puréed fennel and orange, house-made tuna *prosciutto* with Sicilian melon, fresh anchovies with local olive oil, and *scorfano* (an ugly red fish) that tastes delicious, served in a tiny tartlet with a touch of fish roe. This restaurant is simple and truly Italian using fresh, pure local ingredients. The beauty of each dish is that there are fewer than four ingredients in each. Taste the flavors of food. Bravo Riccardo, one of the best meals of the trip!!!!

Let Us Pray

(the only prayer you need to know)

Dio mi guardi da chi non beve vino:

"God, please protect me from those who do not drink wine."

Let us Sing

Vela

By Eli Rallo

Verse:

So close to reality

But so far away

I'm lost in this little town

Each and every day

Let me know when you

Find a place like here back home

Till then

I'm not coming back from Rome

Chorus:

Cause this city is too big and my town is

Too small

Maybe one day I will give you a call

I open my eyes to the hills stretched out wide

Maybe god created a place like this to savor

Do me a favor
And keep the smells
The sound
The beautiful sights
All the same

Verse:
So close to all my friends
And so far away
Maybe sometimes it's good that way
Let me know when you find a place like
Here back home
Till than I'm not coming
Back from Rome

Chorus:
Cause this city is too big and my town is
Too small
Maybe one day I will give you a call
I open my eyes to the hills stretched out wide
Maybe god created a place like this to savor
Do me a favor
And keep the smells
The sound
The beautiful sights

All the same

Bridge:
Raise that glass high
There's no chance to sigh
Love fills the air
I can go without a care
Yeah!

Chorus:
Cause this city is too big and my town is
Too small
Maybe one day I will give you a call
I open my eyes to the hills stretched out wide
Maybe god created a place like this to savor
Do me a favor
And keep the smells
The sound
The beautiful sights
All the same

SATURDAY AUGUST 20, 2011

DAY 7

A LOT OF THINGS CHANGE WHEN YOU'RE ON A BOAT. I DRINK FRENCH wine, I go to the bathroom overboard, I rarely shower, and I rave about a French Rose:

WINE #10

CHATEAU RASQUE ROSÉ

2010

OPPOSITE: Bow to stern, Alpha Centuri.

ABOVE: Fifteen meter jump, Isola di Elba.

OPPOSITE: Cantina at Abbazia di Novacella.

Anna asks if I would like to try a French Rose with lunch, I immediately say "yes" and she pours Kari and me a glass. The wine bursts with fruit and finishes perfectly dry with crisp acidity. This wine is better than either of the two Italian rosati wines I packed for our trip. Thanks Anna, for some mouth-watering French advice.

Today, we must speak of evolution and how all things change over time. I have changed. Some of that hard edge is gone; the corners are rounded a bit, so much so that I think I can probably roll. My wife, Kari, well she is crazy about everything from kids to food to high dives…everything. That hasn't changed, but we are working on her, and hopefully by the end of this trip her anxiousness will subside.

Today, she let all of us (Eli, Jake, Jack and I) jump off a fifteen meter cliff: I never thought that would happen! Maybe my hunch is correct! As always, she looks and feels great. The kids are unbelievable, becoming young adults, with passion and pride. I think our job as parents is being done well, but we continue to take each day in stride, recognizing that it is a long journey.

Evolution is important when drinking and speaking about wine. It is how we mark things from time to time, year to year. Tonight with Anna and Bruno, we will drink a vertical progression of Martin del Nero 2007-2008-2009. We have just anchored in Calanova, a small bay with a quaint, beautiful setting; offshore breezes are blowing and things feel just fine. We will take the dinghy to the small dock located on the beach. Ristorante Calanova is located in one of the five beach homes in this tiny village.

Anna asks the owner of Ristorante Calanova if we could bring some of the wines I brought on board the boat to dinner. She tells them I am writing a travelogue of the wines and food we eat on our trip through Tuscany. They happily agree, and the mood is immediately set. I open all three bottles of Martin del Nero to give them time to breathe and open up. Often times, we forget that wine is in the bottle for three to five years, sometimes fifteen years or more. Give the wine time; let it come to the party. Its magic lies in the bottle, but it hasn't fully arrived until it is in the glass.

WINE #11

MATTEO CORREGGIA ARNEIS

2010

WINE #12

ABBAZIA DI NOVACELLA GEWÜRZTRAMINER

2010

While we wait for Martin del Nero and the food to arrive, I order two bottles of Vini Bianchi: a 2010 Matteo Correggia Arneis from Piemonte and Abbazia di Novacella Gewürztraminer 2010, from Alto Adige. The Arneis is good, as expected. The 2010 vintage was very good for whites in Piemonte. Even though Piemonte is known for the king of all red wines in Italy, Barolo, it is also the source of some exceptional, inexpensive white wines.

On the white side tonight, the Gewürztraminer really stands out. The violets on the nose of the Abbazia wine were amazing almost like a spray of perfume. If I were going out dancing, I would definitely sprinkle a little on my neck. The girls would love it. The first sip bursts with sweet peaches and that beautiful minerality of Northern Italian white wines. This wine is a keeper, and for the price it is a perfect ten. Drink this wine now; this is a Summer white wine, period…

Let's not forget that the great Monk, Martin Del Nero, is at the party too. After tasting the whites, we decide (we being myself, Captain Bruno, and the remarkable Anna) to taste the three Martin del Nero wines before dinner. We are all having fresh caught fish of some species or another for dinner and these wines will definitely overpower the food.

WINE #13

MARTIN DEL NERO

2007

WINE #14

MARTIN DEL NERO

2008

WINE #15

MARTIN DEL NERO

2009

The 2007 vintage is interesting. I am slightly concerned when I pull the cork. It is very easy to pull and has a wine line that almost hits the capsule. This can mean that air has come in contact with the wine and it is beginning to oxidize. Luckily, I think we have just made it. The wine is intact and drinking very well. I would say this is a drink NOW wine; it is reaching its peak. It has great syrupy cherry fruit, nice soft tannins, and the

ABOVE: Victor and Anna Lisa Tempesti in front of "Resta."

elegant beauty of Anna Lisa Tempesti. Again, drink it now. This wine is probably the most enjoyable of all three for consumption today and, yes, we consume it.

The 2008 vintage is the best wine of the vertical for me. The wine has stature, standing tall like Lady Liberty in the New York harbor. The wine has all the fruit notes of Sangiovese on the nose — cherry, wild berries, and some flinty minerality. The complexity runs deep, with layers of oak tannins and beautiful ageability, probably an eight to twelve year wine. I taste this wine several times through the evening and it gets better as it opens and aerates. The 2008 bottle of Martin Del Nero is happy to be at our dinner party on the beach at Calanova.

The 2009 vintage, which is Anna Lisa's current vintage, is still a baby. I must say that the aromatics of this wine are sensational. It really blows me away. The nose bursts with cherry, plums, and berries that are in balance with the firm tannins and crisp acidity. Unlike the 2008 that is drinkable at a young age, the 2009 needs more time in the bottle. I love tasting and drinking verticals of good wine. For me, drinking wines in a chronological sequence is one of the most important ways to enhance your knowledge of wine, and in particular, the evolution of wine.

The final results are in from our tasting at Calanova:

Anna –   2007 Martin del Nero

Bruno –   2009 Martin del Nero

Vic –   2008 Martin del Neo

Listen up! Do not miss the food at Ristorante Calanova: fresh caught fish, alive immediately prior to cooking, prepared perfectly, simply, and served at your table on the beach. Clearly, white wine is the choice for this evening but not a bad place to drink a vertical of Martin del Nero (MDN), either.

MDN 90 POINTS MATURE

2007

MDN 95 POINTS YOUNG

2008

MDN 92 POINTS YOUNG

2009

Ristorante Calanova – Mind Blowing Simplicity. 100 points
Locale Calanova
Isola d' Elba
www.ristorantecalanova.it

SUNDAY AUGUST 21, 2001

DAY 8

WINE #16

DAL FORNO VALPOLICELLA SUPERIORE

2005

BOTTARGA IS DRIED TUNA ROE, A SPECIALTY OF THE ITALIAN ISLANDS
Sardegna and Siciliy. *Bottarga* is a long, fat roe sac salted and massaged
by hand over a several-week period to preserve it. After this process is

ABOVE: From the bow looking to the stern, Alpha Centuri.

complete the roe is pressed between wood planks that are weighted by stones and sun dried for one or two months, depending on the roe and the producer. *Bottarga* has a lively, salty, very sharp flavor. It is best served with *linguine*, really good olive oil, garlic, and Italian parsley. This batch of *bottarga* came from a fisherman friend of Anna's in Sardegna. This is traditional, authentic, and typical Italian food. *Bottarga* ranges in price, depending on the quality. Some consider it the poor man's caviar.

Anna asks if we want to eat on the boat this evening. I say sure, why not? Anna is a very good, I mean very good cook. She used to be the private chef for Paul Allen, of Microsoft. Anna says the kids will eat pasta with a *Bolognese* sauce that she made from the fresh roast beef she served to us for lunch. We will have *linguini con bottarga* with local olive oil, garlic and parsley. Now this is an interesting pairing: a red wine from arguably one of the great Italian wine producers, Romano Dal Forno, with Anna's bottarga pasta. I can't wait.

We start dinner with a *piccolo* (small) local watermelon with fresh tomato, mint, and olive oil salad, fresh Elba figs and white peaches – *fior di latte mozzarella* – and *schiacciata* (local bread) with anchovies. I prepare the antipasti in the tight, but adequate, kitchen of the boat. Tonight, we start with an Italian rosato from Puglia. It is good, but not great wine; all the same on a perfect summer night. The wine also acts as a very good palate cleanser for what is on the tasting schedule. I do not rate this wine. I drink it, but I do not taste it. Is that possible?

We eat and laugh under the starlit sky as the pasta for the *bottarga* cooks, and the Dal Forno Valpolicella opens perfectly (I suggest opening

Dal Forno wines one to two hours before tasting). Anna serves the pasta, as I pour the wine. To be totally honest, I cannot imagine a more perfect evening – great people, great food, and great wine. The lights in the harbor glisten off the *azzurro* blue sea and the twinkle in my wife's eyes make the evening a sure top-ten memory. The wine shows beautifully, with a nose of dried black fruit, plums and blackberries, and a hint of quarry stone on the nose. On the tongue, this fifteen-percent alcohol grandiose wine smacks you with fruit, minerals and soft, but elegant, tannins. You think a wine this big would be overpowering, but quite to the contrary – this wine is elegant and soft, almost unimaginable. The first glass invites a second…

Romano Dal Forno plants the highest density vineyards in Italy, at nearly 12,000 plants per hectare (the norm in Italy is 5,000 plants for hectare). This creates a syrupy concentration in his wines that is unmatched. Add the planting density to his very strict green harvest pruning, and his yields per plant and hectare are amongst the lowest in the world. I can openly say that the standard Valpolicella from Dal Forno is as grand as most Amarones from other producers.

What a pairing: this beautiful fruit forward Valpolicella and the perfectly-cured *tonno bottarga* with *linguini*, a perfect contrast of salt and fruit. It's similar to pairing Prosciutto di Parma with a sweet Sicilian melon or white fig. This is arguably one of the best food and wine pairings I have ever tasted.

DAY 9

Marciana Marina on Isola di Elba is a beautiful old port with a classic seaside village.

I must take a swim to shore. The water shimmers as the sun rises. I see my reflection off the water as I stand on the boat. I feel I am looking in a mirror. After several bottles of wine the night before, the plunge immediately refreshes me. I swim to a black sand beach adjacent to the beautiful, colorful, historic, stone buildings on the main street adjacent to the port. This is a good start to the day.

Eat at:

Ristorante Publius – great, great view – good food – impolite, random service

Capo al Piano – Pizzeria and spaghetti

La Scaletta – Pizzeria, local food

WINE #17

FONTODI FLACCIANELLO DELLA PIEVE

1999

After dinner, it is time to DIVE back into wine! This wine has been voted the top red wine of Italy two times in the past decade, and deservedly so. The bottle we open on the boat is twelve years old and in very nice shape. I decide to decant it, which turns out to be a very good choice. We use Bruno's magical decanter. It is an old, cracked decanter that Bruno had repaired with some type of green epoxy. The decanter looks like a magical old Genie bottle. The wine is beautiful, the air fresh, and the lights glimmer from Marina Marciana; not a bad way to drink a twelve-year old wine. Everyone should try this in his or her lifetime.

Giovanni Manetti, the young winemaker at Flaccianello, is a genius who truly believes in Sangiovese. Not only does he believe in Sangiovese, but he believes in growing it organically. His wine is truly an achievement, especially considering that the nature of Sangiovese is fickle and that his

vineyards have no chemical intervention. None!

The wine has scents of dried red fruit, cherry, *fragola* (strawberries), and berries. It almost has a Burgundian feel on the nose. Anna and Bruno spent some time in Dijon and drank a lot of Burgundy those days. They put this thought into my head and I have to agree: Sangiovese and Pinot Noir in the same sentence. That may be a first from me. The amazing thing about this wine is the finish — firm tannins, and a balanced acidity, but the fruit… bang, right to the end of your breath. This bottle was a cherry (no pun intended), and one of the best I had opened thus far on the trip.

When you drink great wine, it makes everything better. As I sit on the deck of the boat, I do not know if this could get any better. Wine is a spirit that thrills you; it moves you, and it transcends time. Wine is born in a bottle, but comes to life in a glass, and it always makes a party a blast. So sit back and enjoy. Maybe the world will unravel, but wine will fix it all, one glass at a time! That is my promise…

MATTEOCORREGGIA

2010

ROERO ARNEIS

DENOMINAZIONE DI ORIGINE
CONTROLLATA E GARANTITA

BRUNELLO
DI MONTALCINO

DENOMINAZIONE DI ORIGINE CONTROLLATA E GARANTITA

RED WINE - PRODUCT OF ITALY

COL D'ORCIA

BOTTLED BY TENUTA COL D'ORCIA S.p.A. - MONTALCINO - ITALIA

FLACCIANELLO
DELLA PIEVE

IMBOTTIGLIATO ALL'ORIGINE NELLA
AZIENDA AGRICOLA FONTODI
DI GIOVANNI E MARCO MANETTI S.S.
PANZANO - ITALIA

COLLI TOSCANA CENTRALE
INDICAZIONE GEOGRAFICA TIPICA

75 cl e
750 ml e
PRODUCE OF ITALY
RED TABLE WINE

Uccelliera

Rosso di
MONTALCINO

DENOMINAZIONE DI ORIGINE CONTROLLATA

Poggio Antico

brunello
di montalcino

denominazione di origine
controllata e garantita.
Imbottigliato all'ori
gine dalla Società
Agricola Poggio Antico Srl
Montalcino (Siena) Italia

e 13,5%vol

ITALIA

Casanova di Neri

TENUTA NUOVA

BRUNELLO DI MONTALCINO
DENOMINAZIONE DI ORIGINE CONTROLLATA E GARANTITA

BRUNELLO DI MONTALCINO
DENOMINAZIONE DI ORIGINE CONTROLLATA E GARANTITA

BIONDI-SANTI

MARCA   PROPRIA

TENUTA "GREPPO"

Imbottigliato all'origine dal viticultore
FRANCO BIONDI SANTI
NELLA CANTINA DELLA TENUTA "GREPPO"
MONTALCINO-ITALIA

CHATEAU RASOUE

L'ENFANT DES VIGNES

TARADEAU

MARTIN DEL NERO

fattoria resta

Uccelliera

BRUNELLO di
MONTALCINO

DENOMINAZIONE DI ORIGINE CONTROLLATA E GARANTITA

LEMACCHIOLE
BOLGHERI

MESSORIO

Vie di Romans
CHARDONNAY

VIE DI ROMANS

Guidalberto

TOSCANA
INDICAZIONE GEOGRAFICA TIPICA
IMBOTTIGLIATO DA
TENUTA SAN GUIDO
BOLGHERI - ITALIA
L. 037 - 02

ED WINE
RODUCT OF ITALY

Alc. 13.5% by v
NET CONT. 750 M

Ribolla
2004

MOVIA

SINCE 1820
B R D A

*Vintage
Tunina*

DAY 10

Ristorante L'Ostrica – Luciano

Localita Forno

Porto Ferraio

Isola d'Elba

www.ristorantelostica.com

Phone: 348 6048355

A GREAT MEAL... PERIOD. HERE ARE SOME OF THE HIGHLIGHTS:

<u>Sardine Fresche</u> – Fresh caught Sardines, lightly grilled, with extra

virgin olive oil and local sea salt, BANG! Just great.

Cozze Ripieni – Fresh mussels stuffed with the soft inner pieces of Tuscan bread, with olive oil and seasoning, then cooked in fresh tomato sauce. The sauce thickened from the bread, the flavors of the sea sublime. I had three orders. I will say no more...

Calamari Ripieni - Local calamari stuffed with mussels, shrimp, clam, and a little bread cooked for 2 hours in tomato sauce then sliced in silver dollar sized morsels. Yum, Yum, Yum.

Branzino Grigliato – Fresh whole *branzino*, grilled with sea salt and olive oil, filleted at the table and served with potatoes and baby local tomatoes. Fresh, Fresh, Fresh. So fresh, I thought the fish was going to talk back!

WINE #18

MOVIA RIBOLLA

2008

I am an Italian wine snob, and I drink Movia wine, despite the fact that it is only half-Italian. Movia winery is officially in Slovenia, but its vineyards straddle Friuli in Northeastern Italy. Movia wines are given the appellation of Brda, the Slovenian name for Collio.

Ales Kristancic, owner and winemaker at Movia, is part genius, part madman, and a great winemaker. His white wines are aged in large

Slovenian casks and Slovenian barriques which are slightly smaller than French barrique barrels. Ales leaves his white wines on the lees, in contact with the yeast, for up to two years, without stirring or handling. His wines are totally in sync with nature. They are all fined and filtered, governed by the atmospheric pressure incurred by the arrival of a new moon.

I would highly recommend this wine with fish, but not just any fish — only pure fish. What do I mean? In the United States, most cooks, chefs, moms, and dads overcook fish and/or cover it with a layer of glop: not good... In Italy, especially on the islands, the fish is fresh, caught that day and the preparation is simple: grilled or oven roasted, with local olive oil and sea salt and that's it! *Voila*! I ate a lot of fish. All of the descriptions are listed above and this wine is a perfect guest to invite to the meal.

The Movia Ribolla is very interesting and unique, which makes it beautiful to me. On the nose, peaches, apricots, and white flowers provide complexity and depth that are unmatched. I would say exotic, just like Ales, the master of Movia.

WINE #19

JERMANN VINTAGE TUNINA

2008

Silvio Jermann changed the way the world views Italian white wines. He was one of the first to prove the ageability of Northern Italian white wines. I have tasted many vintages of Vintage Tunina, but tonight the 2008 Vintage Tunina is magnificent. The layers of fruit, apricots, nectarines, and white figs remind me of a high-end fruit salad. The complexity has a backbone of mountain minerals and the undeniable acidity of Jermann wines that is a genetic trait of his terroir. Vintage Tunina is a blend of Sauvignon, Chardonnay, Ribolla Gialla, Malvasia, and Picolit of which some of the grapes are harvested very late, magnifying the ripe fruit of this wine. The great part about Vintage Tunina is you can drink it now or cellar it, and it will evolve beautifully for the next ten years.

Uccelliera Brunello di Montalcino Riserva (First Riserva Vintage)

1997

Andrea handed me a bottle of the 1997 Riserva in a VinniBag (a specially-designed, sealed bag approved for travel on airplanes). I know this wine is not destined to make it back to New Jersey. This was Andrea's first Riserva vintage, of which very few bottles remain. He is a good and very generous friend, so I accepted the gift with a big hug and a kiss. For those of you who know me, I am like a kid on payday. If there is money in my pocket, I want to spend it. Likewise, if there is wine in my possession, I want to drink it, enjoy it, and share it.

I have had this bottle of Riserva for eight days now and I have been dying to cut open the bag and let the magic escape. That is exactly what I did on the night of August 23, 2011; this bottle will accompany us to Ristorante L'Ostrica for dinner tonight. I decide to drink the wine after we eat, since we all order fresh fish of one variety or another. The waiter offers a decanter and I accept. I decant the wine and decide it will be perfect for dessert. A fourteen-year old Brunello will make a scrumptious after dinner treat. I hope!

I always have high expectations for Andrea's wines. Some of the best Brunellos I have ever tasted are from Uccelliera. The Uccelliera 1997 Riserva will not disappoint us. The wine is ready to drink and in great form. If I had some of this wine in my cellar, I would drink the rest of it over the next five years. What I love about this wine is its persistence: fruit, syrupy cherries, smooth, elegant, and tame, but with ample tannins. This puppy evolved beautifully.

Recently, Antonio Galloni of The Wine Advocate wrote that, "I would be hard-pressed to name another grower who has made such huge strides in recent years as Andrea Cortonesi. The artisan tradition of Montalcino is alive and well in this small, no-frills winery, where the wines have never been better".

DAY 11

THE GROWING SEASON IN BOLGHERI HAD BEEN EXCELLENT UNTIL THE heat wave hit during the first three weeks in August, 2011. Heat is necessary for grapes, however, the temperature for these three weeks was in the mid 90's (too hot) and it did not cool down at night to allow the vines to be refreshed. The constant heat accelerates the natural growth cycle of the grapes causing them to ripen more quickly than usual. Merlot is the earliest ripening of the Bordeaux varietals that are planted in Bolgheri, and is typically harvested before the Cabernet Sauvignon, Cabernet Franc, and Petit Verdot. So on the morning of August 25th, many producers start harvesting merlot from the lowest lying and typically hottest vineyards,

as the grapes begin to show signs of heat stress (shriveling of the grapes). Bolgheri is very busy with tractors pulling trailers with the little red harvesting crates back and forth from the vineyards, creating a sort of New York-style traffic jam in the small town of Bolgheri; beautiful and hectic.

Sebastiano Rosa and I have become great friends. He is the winemaker at Tenuta San Guido and we met, by chance, five years ago during a working trip through New Jersey with his importer, Kobrand. Sarah, the Kobrand representative at the time called and asked me if I had a little time, as they had an hour before their next appointment. I said sure, and she and Sebastiano came to see me.

We tasted all of his wines. Knowing that Sebastiano had been the winemaker at Argiano in Montalcino before going back to work with his family, I began to ask him about Brunello's and the current scandal in Montalcino over the 2003 vintage. Sebastiano quietly tells me that the scandal is very real and that many producers had added non-permitted grapes to their DOCG protected Brunello di Montalcino. We opened a 1999 Valdicava Brunello di Montalcino, and drank the whole bottle, while speaking about Montalcino. We became immediate friends. Each summer during my *Giro* through Italy, my family and I stay with Sebastiano and his wife, Elena, for one week at Tenuta San Guido.

Today starts with lunch at the beach in Bolgheri. Tenuta San Guido owns land (900 acres) from the top of the hill in Bolgheri all the way to the sea. Flor, Sebastiano and Elena's cook, makes us a picnic lunch for the beach. *Tutto bene*! The picnic consists of chicken Milanese, *pomodorini*, *anguria* (watermelon), *mozzarella, foccaccia, Prosciutto di San Danielle*, a few bottles of water and, of course, a bottle of wine.

OPPOSITE: Sunset from the town of Bolgheri.

CONSORZIO DEL VINO BRUNELLO DI MONTALCINO
ELENCO DEI PRODUTTORI ASSOCIATI IMBOTTIGLIATORI
LIST OF MEMBERS BOTTLERS

Area	N.	Azienda - Estate	Brunello	Rosso	Moscadello	Sant'Antimo
C1	10	Abbadia Ardenga	■	■		
B3	69	Agostina Pieri	■	■		■
B1	13	Altesino	■	■		
A3	23	Argiano	■	■		
B2	103	Armilla	■	■		
B2	203	Baccinetti	■	■		
B3	18	Banfi	■	■	■	■
B2	140	Barbi	■	■		
B1	1	Baricci	■	■		
B2	20	Bartoli Giusti Tenuta Comunali	■	■		■
B2	145	Bellaria	■	■		■
C3	200	Belpoggio	■	■		
B2	178	Biondi Santi Franco - Tenuta Greppo	■	■		
B1	187	Bonacchi	■	■		■
B2	132	Brunelli	■	■		
B1	216	Bucine	■	■		
A2	7	Camigliano	■	■	■	■
B3	160	Campi di Fonterenza	■	■		
B3	16	Campogiovanni	■	■		
B1	47	Canalicchio - Pacenti Franco	■	■		
B1	164	Canalicchio di Sopra	■	■		
B2	29	Canneta	■	■		■
B1	90	Cantina di Montalcino	■	■		
B1	33	Capanna	■	■	■	■
B3	100	Capanne Ricci	■	■		
B1	17	Caparzo	■	■	■	■
B2	107	Caprili	■	■	■	■
B2	99	Casa Raia	■	■		
C1	48	Casanova di Neri	■	■		
B1	51	Casanuova delle Cerbaie	■	■		
B2	14	Case Basse	■			
B2	58	Casisano Colombaio	■	■		
A2	9	Castelgiocondo e Luce della Vite	■	■		
B2	15	Castelli Martinozzi	■	■		
C3	204	Castello di Velona	■	■		
B2	42	Castello Romitorio	■	■		
B1	183	Castello Tricerchi	■	■		
A1	4	Castiglion del Bosco	■	■		
B1	31	Celestino Pecci	■	■		
B1	59	Cerbaia	■	■		
C2	25	Cerbaiona	■	■		
B3	193	Ciacci Piccolomini d'Aragona	■	■		■
C1	172	Citille di Sopra	■	■		
B3	34	Col d'Orcia	■	■		
C1	206	Col di Lamo	■	■		
C2	142	Coldisole	■	■		
A2	162	Collelceto	■	■		
B3	114	Collemattoni	■	■		
B1	144	Colleoni	■	■		
B2	209	Colombaio	■	■		
B3	56	Conte Placido	■			
C1	212	Cordella	■	■		
B2	129	Corte Pavone	■	■		
B2	35	Costanti	■	■		
A2	153	Cupano	■	■		■
A2	220	Domus Vitae	■	■	■	■
B1	155	Donatella Cinelli Colombini	■	■		
B2	158	Donna Olga	■	■		
C2	30	Fanti	■	■		■
B1	5	Fastelli	■	■		
B2	102	Fattoi	■	■		
B3	79	Ferrero	■	■		
B2	126	Ferro	■	■		
B2	85	Fontebuia	■			
C2	191	Fornacella	■	■		
C2	122	Fornacina	■	■		
B2	95	Fossacolle	■	■		
B2	12	Fuligni	■	■		
C2	57	Gianni Brunelli - Le Chiuse di Sotto	■	■		
B2	55	Greppino		■		
B2	151	Il Cocco	■	■		
B2	19	Il Colle	■	■		
B1	210	Il Colombaio	■	■		
B2	91	Il Forteto del Drago	■	■		
B3	40	Il Grappolo – Fortius	■	■		
B1	163	Il Marroneto	■	■		
B1	157	Il Palazzone	■			
B1	161	Il Paradiso di Frassina	■			■
B1	36	Il Paradiso di Manfredi	■	■		
B3	2	Il Patrizio	■	■		
B2	52	Il Poggiolo	■	■	■	
B3	2	Il Poggione	■	■	■	■
B2	133	Il Valentiano	■			
C1	134	Innocenti	■	■		
B2	180	L' Aietta	■	■		
B1	32	La Campana	■	■		
C2	152	La Collina dei Lecci	■	■		
C3	115	La Colombina	■	■		■
B2	80	La Croce	■			
C2	74	La Fiorita	■	■		
C2	125	La Fornace	■	■		
C1	112	La Fortuna	■	■		■
B1	39	La Gerla	■	■		
C2	37	La Lecciaia	■	■		■
B2	123	La Magia	■	■		
B1	62	La Mannella	■	■		
B2	84	La Melina			■	
C3	54	La Palazzetta	■	■		■
C3	121	La Pieve	■	■		
C2	53	La Poderina	■	■	■	
C2	106	La Rasina	■	■		
C2	109	La Serena	■	■		
B2	60	La Togata	■	■		
B2	65	La Torre	■	■		
C3	49	La Velona	■	■		■
B1	44	Lambardi	■	■		■
C1	146	Lazzeretti	■	■		
B1	73	Le Chiuse	■	■		
B1	108	Le Gode	■	■		
C2	46	Le Macioche	■	■		
C3	137	Le Presi	■	■		
B2	188	Le Ragnaie	■	■		
C3	128	Le 7 Camicie	■			
B3	3	Lisini	■	■		
C2	113	Luciani	■	■		■
A2	61	Marchesato degli Aleramici	■	■		
C2	21	Mastrojanni	■	■		■
B2	195	Máté	■	■		■
B2	92	Mocali	■	■		■
B1	118	Molinari Carlo	■	■		■
C3	131	Molino di Sant'Antimo	■	■		■
B1	147	Montecarbello	■			
B2	63	Padelletti	■	■		
C2	71	Palazzo	■	■		
C3	218	Panizzi	■			
B1	213	Paradisone - Colle degli Angeli	■	■		■
B2	202	Parisi Domenico	■	■		
B2	211	Passo del Lume Spento	■	■		
B1	167	Pian delle Querci	■	■		■
A2	104	Pian delle Vigne	■			
B2	116	Pian di Macina	■	■		
B3	70	Piancornello	■	■		■
B2	86	Pietroso	■	■		
B2	76	Pieve Santa Restituta	■			
B1	190	Pinino	■	■		
B2	97	Piombaia	■	■		■
B2	149	Podere Brizio - Roberto Bellini	■	■		■
B1	192	Podere Canalino	■	■		
C1	214	Podere Canapaccia	■	■		
C1	173	Podere La Vigna	■	■		
C2	219	Podere Le Ripi	■	■		
C1	185	Podere Paganico	■	■		
B1	208	Podere San Giacomo Soc. Agr. SS	■	■		
B3	143	Poderuccio	■	■		
B1	94	Poggiarellino	■	■		
B2	8	Poggio Antico	■	■		
B3	11	Poggio degli Ulivi	■	■		
B2	186	Poggio dell'Aquila	■	■		
C3	67	Poggio di Sotto	■	■		
C2	141	Poggio Il Castellare	■	■		■
B2	215	Poggio Rubino	■	■		
B2	207	Querce Bettina	■	■		
B2	22	Quercecchio	■	■		
C1	199	Rendola	■	■		
C1	177	Renieri	■	■		
A2	27	Riguardo	■	■		

ZONA DI PRODUZIONE CON UBICAZIONE DELLE AZIENDE IMBOTTIGLIATRICI
PRODUCTION AREA AND SITE OF BOTTLING ESTATES

B2	175	S. Lucia	■	■		
B2	38	Salvioni	■	■		
C2	179	San Filippo	■	■	■	
B2	130	San Lorenzo	■	■	■	
C2	174	San Polino	■	■	■	
C2	75	San Polo	■	■		
B2	169	SanCarlo	■	■		
C1	148	Santa Giulia	■	■		
B1	24	Sassetti	■	■		
B1	6	Sassetti Livio - Pertimali	■	■	■	
C1	205	Sassodisole	■	■		
B1	127	Scopetino	■			
B1	28	Scopetone	■	■		
B2	154	Scopone	■	■	■	
B3	139	Sesta di Sopra	■	■		
B3	89	Sesti	■	■		
B1	26	Siro Pacenti	■	■		
B2	111	Società Agricola Bolsignano	■	■		
B2	68	Solaria	■	■		
B3	138	Talenti	■	■		
B2	197	Tassi	■	■	■	
B1	77	Tenimenti Angelini - Val di Suga	■	■	■	
B2	124	Tenuta Crocedimezzo	■	■	■	
B3	83	Tenuta di Collosorbo	■	■	■	
B3	82	Tenuta di Sesta	■	■	■	
B2	78	Tenuta Greppone Mazzi	■			
A2	159	Tenuta La Fuga	■	■		
B1	176	Tenuta La Torraccia	■	■		
B2	135	Tenuta Le Potazzine	■	■		
C3	166	Tenuta Oliveto	■	■		
C3	194	Tenuta San Giorgio	■	■		
C1	117	Tenuta Vitanza	■	■		
B2	217	Tenuta Vittoria	■	■		
B2	45	Tenute Friggiali e Pietranera	■	■		
C3	105	Tenute Niccolai - Podere Bellarina	■	■		
C1	201	Tenute Piccini srl	■	■		
A1	81	Tenute Silvio Nardi	■	■	■	■
C2	150	Terralsole	■	■		
B1	189	Terre Nere	■	■		
B2	50	Tiezzi	■	■	■	
B2	110	Tornesi	■	■		
C3	66	Uccelliera	■	■		
B1	43	Valdicava	■	■	■	
C3	96	Vasco Sassetti	■	■	■	
B2	88	Ventolaio	■	■		
C2	136	Verbena	■	■	■	
B2	119	Villa a Tolli	■	■		
B2	98	Villa I Cipressi	■	■		
B2	101	Villa Le Prata	■	■	■	
B2	168	Villa Poggio Salvi	■	■	■	■
B3	171	Vini Italiani da Sogno	■	■		
C3	221	Voliero	■	■		

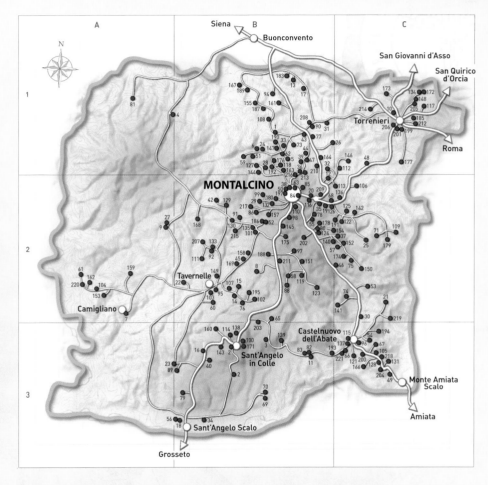

Produttori imbottigliatori
Members bottlers   Totale - Total   **208**

Superficie totale del territorio di Montalcino
Total surface covered by the township of Montalcino   **Ha 24.000**

Superficie dei terreni vitati - Surface covered with vineyards
Totale - Total   **Ha 3.500**

Brunello di Montalcino DOCG   Ha   2.100
Rosso di Montalcino DOC   Ha   510
Moscadello di Montalcino DOC   Ha   50
Sant'Antimo DOC   Ha   480
Altri vini - other wines   Ha   360

71

GRATTAMACCO VERMENTINO

2009

Grattamacco Vermentino is the house white wine of Sebastiano and Elena. I only drink it in Bolgheri because it is hard to find at home, and I savor every sip. Believe me, lunch doesn't get better than this. Lunch is *de rigore* at Tenuta San Guido, but for me there is nothing like lunch on the beach. Afterwards, I take a two-hour nap under a thatched hut on the beach, with the ocean rumbling me to sleep. Last night was a 2 am wine and food extravaganza, and I desperately need this nap. I am awakened by my children, as they jump on top of me to wake me for my next appointment, Tenuta Ornellaia at 3 pm.

Ornellaia is a relatively new winery dating back to the late 1980's. Initially, the winery was owned by Lodovico Antinori. He later sold a fifty-percent to the Frescobaldi family. In my estimation Antinori made a huge mistake by selling his remaining fifty-percent to the Mondavi family in the 1990's. This partnership would not last for long. The story is told that the Mondavi's had financial trouble and sold their fifty-percent interest to the Frescobaldi family. Today, Tenuta Ornellaia is fully owned by the Frescobaldi family and has blossomed into one of the best and most important wineries in Italy.

The winery is planted with only Bordeaux varieties: Cabernet Sauvignon, Merlot, Cabernet Franc, and Petit Verdot. Some experts say that these grape

varieties grow better in Bolgheri than anywhere else in the world. When I asked Axel Heinz, the winemaker at Ornellaia this question, he politely did not go quite that far. He did say, "These Bordeaux varieties grow in a much different way than in France." He had one of those confident, yes, smiles on his face as he spoke.

Tenuta Ornellaia is the most beautiful estate that I have ever seen. The property is completely manicured, no blade of grass out of place and recently was outfitted with a brand new, modern winery in the Bolgheri hillside. It is very hard to get into see, but keep trying. It is worth it.

Can you believe it is still Thursday?

ABOVE: Mirror mirror on the wall.

OPPOSITE: Ornellaia winery.

ORNELLAIA MASSETO BARREL SAMPLE
2009

Axel Heinz meets me in the Cellars of Ornellaia, after I visited the vineyards with Viola, the woman in charge of customer relations. We embrace, hug and kiss then we say hello, as we had met this spring in New York at an Ornellaia event in Lincoln Center. Axel says to me, "Since you came such a long way to say hello, we have to taste something memorable." I know that I am in for a treat...

RIGHT: Masseto barrel room.

Sometimes when you visit a winery it does not work out. Today, my expectations are not high, as the harvest has just begun in Bolgheri and the *vendemmia* is now the winemaker's most important project. Nature has done its job. It is now the winemaker's job to put the grapes into the bottle, so to speak. Luckily my appointment is at 3 pm, the hottest part of the day. They have suspended the harvest until 5 pm because of the ninety-five degree heat, so Axel was free to meet with me. Bravo, I love the heat!!!

As we talk, we work our way through the barrel rooms and end up in the barrel room of Masseto, which houses a library collection of every vintage of Masseto ever made, some twenty-three vintages. Axel grabs some glasses and a ladro di vino (wine thief) and proclaims, "We will barrel sample the 2009 Masseto." I want to raise my fist and say, "Yes, Yes, Yes!" Instead I say quietly, "That would be great." Masseto is considered by the pundits to be Italy's equivalent to Chateau Petrus.

Axel is surprisingly generous with his wine considering there are only 30,000 bottles of Masseto produced in a typical year. I ask Axel about the 2009 vintage. He tells me that it is his biggest surprise since 2005 when he started at Ornellaia. It is one of those vintages that he was not sure of at harvest time. As the aging process continued (the 2009 had five more months in the barrel prior to bottling), the wine began to develop beautifully.

"Merlot grows differently in Bolgheri than in France," Axel said (Axel had studied and had done his first work in France). Merlot ripens later in Pomerol and has a totally different structure and taste profile. Open a bottle of Masseto and a good bottle of wine from Pomerol and you will

taste first hand Italy vs. France. There have been many tastings throughout France and Italy comparing those wines. Such a tasting, on a personal level, can be quite expensive, but worthwhile.

The 2009 is all about balance and harmony. Typically, young Masseto is too big and muscular for my taste buds. Masseto 2009 is different, still full of tannins and fruit, but surrounded by harmonious elegance. This wine is softer and rounder, reminding me more of Masseto's earlier vintages.

This wine is very approachable in its youth. However, if you plan to cellar this wine, do not drink this wine young (even though it is probably be better than most wines you would open). I would cellar it for eight to fifteen years, and I guarantee that you will be happy if you listen to me and show patience. Yes, I am being like your pain in the ass mother – patience, patience, patience. Axel, thanks for your time and the Masseto treat!

OPPOSITE: Sunset from Castagneto Carducci.

DAY 12

WINE #23

PODERE SAPAIO VOLPOLO (FIRST VINTAGE)

2003

MASSIMO PICCIN HAS BEEN MAKING WINE IN BOLGHERI FOR JUST OVER eight years. I meet him at his home in Bolgheri with my two boys, Jack and Jake. My wife, Kari, and my daughter, Eli, are in Forte dei Marmi with

Sebastiano's wife, Elena, to buy handmade clogs and boots. I definitely need a drink; they have my AMEX card, OUCH! On the bright side, Massimo and I have time to catch up, taste the new vintages of Podere Sapaio, and eat a beautiful light lunch Massimo-style.

I have been a fan of Massimo's wines since I first tasted them five years ago, and I am not the only one. His big wine, Sapaio, receives rave reviews and three consecutive years of <u>Gambero Rosso</u>, Tre Bicchieri. All of the wines we tasted together are exceptional. Like Massimo, I believe the Sapaio 2008 is the best wine he has ever made. We will do a lot of drinking today: champagne from France, Volpolo, Sapaio, cask samples, and finally, several hours later a surprise tasting of Podere Sapaio Volpolo 2003, Massimo's first vintage.

Massimo and a friend hand-picked his first harvest from the vineyards surrounding his home, and produced this wine completely by hand in a quite archaic fashion. The sorting and crushing of the grapes were done outside of what is now his home on the patio. The fermentation was done in an open fermentation vat in his living room, and the barrel aging took place in what is now his dining room. The total production for 2003 Volpolo was a mere 800 bottles. When Massimo came up from the cellar with the bottle he said "There have been some bad ones and some good ones. Let's hope for the best."

Massimo opens the bottle, feels and smells the cork, and pours a little

ABOVE: Massimo Piccin.

wine into his glass and gives it a few swirls. He then put his nose in the glass; then bam, right to his mouth. I could see it in his eyes — this was a good bottle. When Massimo spoke, the words were golden, "This is the best bottle I have opened." He then proceeds to pour us each a glass, and we swirl and sip in silence for what feels like five minutes.

The wine is perfect. It is still totally intact and has great color. The nose is amazing, overripe plums almost like prunes, and a musty minerality found in some parts of Bolgheri, depending on the soil composition. What really gets me is the finish, long and complex with signs of freshness and youth. I would not necessarily age this wine any longer because of the circumstances of its production. This tasting proves to me that Podere Sapaio wines will age very well, and Massimo will be with us for a long time.

WINE #24
LE MACCHIOLE MESSORIO
2006

Only 3,000 bottles of the lush Messorio merlot are made per year. Le Macchiole is different from most other producers in Bolgheri. They produce single varietal wines, of the great Bordeaux and Rhone grape varietals, Merlot, Cabernet Franc, Syrah and Cabernet Sauvignon. But instead of blending these grapes, they choose to produce the true expression of the varietal and bottle each grape variety individually. The flagship wine at

Le Macchiole is Paleo a wine made of 100% Cabernet Franc. My favorite wines of Le Macchiole are Scrio 100% Syrah and Messorio 100% Merlot.

I visit Le Macchiole just prior to my appointment with Massimo at Podere Sapaio. Luca, the marketing director at Le Macchiole, leaves me with a bottle of 2006 Messorio. It is like a crisp one-hundred dollar bill burning a hole in my pocket, so to speak.

I have known Massimo for quite a while and ask him if we should open the bottle after lunch. Massimo loves great wine. I knew he would be a great person to taste this wine with and I knew he would say yes. We put it on ice for just a few minutes to offset the heat and then decanted it for thirty minutes. This wine is now ready.

The 2006 Messorio is the best Merlot I have ever tasted from an Italian producer and there are some damn good world-class merlots produced in Italy. This wine is excellent from start to finish, but what really impresses me is the fruit: fresh, ripe and super persistent. Usually, such fruit forward wines lack complexity, but not this time. Messorio 2006 is dense, with granite mineral tone, beautiful perfume, and lush ripe fruit – a complete, balanced wine in perfect harmony. It is a shame not to drink all you have now, but I believe this wine will evolve further for another twelve to fifteen years. So it's your choice: drink it now and be happy, or show some patience and be really happy.

I know Massimo loves the wine too, but it is kind of awkward to ask a producer about a competitor's wine. I just let it go. I hope he is as impressed as I am. As always, thanks for lunch and another great tasting.

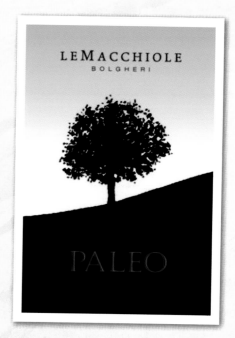

TENUTA SAN GUIDO GUIDALBERTO

2009

This wine is very special and close to my heart. During the summer of 2010, while I was staying at Tenuta San Guido with Sebastiano, I was invited to a tasting with Nicolo' Incisa Della Rocchetta (president Tenuta San Guido), Sebastiano Rosa (winemaker, Guidalberto), Carlo Paoli (general manager, Tenuta San Guido), to choose the blend for Guidalberto 2009.

Sebastiano picked me up from the beach and we met Nicolo' and Carlo at the Tenuta San Guido offices. We walked next store to a guest house on the property and went into the kitchen where the cellar master brought in three beer-type bottles labeled Prova "A", Prova "B", and Prova "C". Sebastiano gave us each three glasses and with a sharpie marker he put an "A" on the base of the first glass, a "B" on the base of the second glass, and a "C" on the base of the third glass. Then he and Carlo poured us each a sample from each bottle in the appropriately labeled glass. The tasting would now begin.

ABOVE: Sebastiano Rosa.

After everyone had tasted through the three samples, a discussion soon began and everyone was speaking Italian. I understand much more Italian than I speak, but after a few minutes Nicolo' demanded that everyone speak English, which they all do very well. I was an important customer there and was also the taste of the United States, their largest market for Tenuta San Guido wines.

There was a short pause and Nicolo' asked about my thoughts on the three samples. I responded by saying, sample "A" was too tannic for the United States market. The wine needed to be in better balance. I thought sample "B" had the best aromatics. It burst with cherries and fresh ripe berries, but it did not have the structure I would have liked behind the supple fruit. Sample "C" had it all — a beautiful nose, fragrant and aromatic, full of ripe black fruit and berries, followed by firm but agreeable tannins and just the right amount of acidity. I then told my tasting partners that "C" was clearly my favorite sample. If possible, I would mix five to ten percent of sample "B" with sample "C" to make a blockbuster wine for the 2009 vintage. The conversation returned to Italian for several minutes and then the results were in: a unanimous decision on sample "C," with the brilliant aromatics of sample "B" close behind. What became the final blend, I cannot say for sure, but based on what I know, I believe that sample "C" became Guidalberto 2009.

These sample bottles were taken from large stainless steel tanks used by the winemaker to blend the individual barrels and varietals to assemble or blend the final product. Shortly after decanting the final blend, the wine is bottled and then stored in the cellar for six to twelve months before

it's released for consumption. Guidalberto 2009 became available in the United States market around March of 2011.

While at Tenuta San Guido this summer, I drink and taste several bottles of Guidalberto 2009 (even the guys who make Sassicaia do not get to drink it every day). I am delighted with the wine's evolution in the bottle and I think this is the best Guidalberto, that Sebastiano and Tenuta San Guido have ever made.

Guidalberto 2009 is lush and elegant. I do not like over oaked-wines, and Sebastiano's use of second- and third-passage oak is brilliant with this vintage. Nature gave him the grapes, and the great winemakers seem to tweak the fullest potential of the grapes when they get them into the cellar. In my mouth the wine is full of wild, sweet strawberries, and elegant refined tannins with a super smooth long finish. This wine is a beautiful stand-alone baby brother of Sassicaia.

On August 31, 2011 just a day after I left Bolgheri, Antonio Galloni of The Wine Advocate, reviewed Guidalberto 2009. Enclosed is the complete review:

OPPOSITE: Guidalberto 2009, samples.

2009 Tenuta San Guido Guidalberto

Tenuta San Guido

A Proprietary Blend Dry Red Table wine from Tuscany, Italy

The Wine Advocate # 196, Aug 2011

Antonio Galloni

92+

Drink: 2012 - 2019

The 2009 Guidalberto flows across the palate with layers of radiant red fruit. This is another striking, supple Guidalberto loaded with personality. Stylistically it is quite close to the 2007, but with perhaps a touch less body but equally silky, polished tannins. Freshly cut roses, spices and a burst of pure red berries add nuance on the finish. Guidalberto is no longer the stunning value it once was, but it is quite gorgeous in this vintage just the same. This is easily one of the best vintages I can recall tasting. Guidalberto is 60% Cabernet Sauvignon and 40% Merlot. Anticipated maturity: 2012-2019.

Tenuta San Guido is on a roll these days. Over the last few years, the estate has released a number of hugely delicious wines. These new releases are nicely aligned with their respective vintages. The entry-level Le Difese and Guidalberto both capture the essence of a sunny year that made wines well suited to near-term drinking, while the 2008 Sassicaia captures the potential of a powerful vintage characterized by low yields and a late harvest.

Galloni, Antonio. "A Proprietary Blend Dry Red Table Wine from Tuscany, Italy." The Wine Advocate 196 (August 2011) Print.

DAY 14

The Last Night:
La Pineta Ristorante
Marina di Bibbona, Tuscany
00390586600016

FOR THE LAST THREE YEARS AT THE END OF OUR TRIP, I INVITE MY
friends from Tuscany to dinner at La Pineta Restaurant. An apropos thank
you and good bye for our friends who take time from their busy lives to
take care of my family and me. I have been astonished each time at the

freshness and quality of the fish and seasonal ingredients. Tonight, I am sure there will be more of the same.

La Pineta is located on the beach Marina di Bibbona, in the Livorno province of Tuscany. It is near Castagneto Carducci and Bolgheri, home to many great wines. It is accessible through a road that crosses a deep, natural forest from which the restaurant takes its name La Pineta (the pine).

The restaurant began as a small house by the sea. Its structure remains as it originally was built – mostly wood, with the window sashes painted light blue. Seating consists of a large room with very few tables and a little patio overlooking the sea.

Originally, the restaurant served simple fish dishes rooted in the traditions of Livorno. In the 1980's, Luciano started to work with his parents managing the restaurant, but never stopped his main love, fishing. In 1996 Luciano took over the management and day to day operations of the restaurant. He still owns three fishing boats that provide him with the "*materie prime*" for his recipes, fresh fish of the local Tyrrhenian coast.

Luciano's fishing experience and knowledge of fish allows him to experiment with fresh fish recipes. He continually reinterprets the local recipes and Tuscan tradition, by introducing new ingredients and original ideas. The simplicity of the food and flavors is the key to his tremendous success.

I hate suits, sport coats, and ties. If any of these items are mandatory attire at a restaurant, I am usually not going. How do you unwind, relax, enjoy family, friends, food, and wine with a tie around your neck? Downright impossible! Tonight I will eat in shorts, a linen shirt and flip flops. Ahhhhhhh!

Luciano's restaurant was awarded One Michelin Star. Can you imagine that? Quite honestly, it may be the best fish restaurant in the world. I have eaten in many restaurants in my travels. I have tasted some great food and wine, but never have I eaten such great food in such a relaxed, casual atmosphere. Bravo, Well Done, Luciano!!!

La Pineta has wood floors, white tablecloths, and its windows and doors are open to the sea. It is fresh…it is spiritual…it is unique. When I walk in, I immediately know it is going to be great. The smell, the vibe and, of course, Luciano, who darted for the door when he sees Elena and Sebastiano. Hugs and kisses, of course. Then, the best table in the house right by the sea. At La Pineta you do not order. You leave that in the hands of Luciano. He knows his fish and will serve you the best. Why should tonight be any different?

Sebastiano orders:

WINE #26

VIE DI ROMANS CHARDONNAY

2009

… and that would be the wine of choice for tonight. A great fish wine with medium body and complexity; it goes perfectly with Luciano's simple seafood creations. By the way, Luciano has a great wine list and cellar. As I expect, Luciano orders for me. My only words to Luciano are: "make me whatever you think I should eat. By the way, I am hungry." Everyone ate, but I really ate.

Here is tonight's menu: (in Italian with English interpretation):

Millefoglie di baccala' mantecato con vellutata di porri

Millefeuille of creamed salt cod with veloute sauce

Spaghetti alle vongole veraci

Spaghetti with clam sauce

Straccetti di pasta fresca

Homemade pasta squares with red mullet sauce

Cacciucco in oliocottura

Olive oil cooked fresh fish stew

Millefoglie con crema pasticcera e carmelo

Millefeuille with custard and carmel

TOP: Luciano Zazzeri.

ABOVE: Pasta with Red Mullet at La Pineta.

LEFT: Crudo, La Pineta.

Oh yeah, the title: if you ever go to Elba you will understand. The place is absolutely beautiful, the landscape, the sea, the people. This is not Siberia, and after checking out Napoleon's castle, prison, whatever you want to call it, he was definitely not exiled, in the literal sense. He lived happily during his "exile" on Isola di Elba.

OPPOSITE: Captain America on the beach in Bolgheri.

SPECIAL THANKS TO:

My wife, Kari, and my children Eli, Jake, & Jack	
"The Professor" Anthony Verdoni	Mentor, Editor & Friend
Preston Porter "Presto-Matic"	Editor & Print Coordinator
Thomas Shebell	Final Editor & Friend Extraordinary
Timothy Hall	Editor
Alpha Centuri	Bruno and Anna
Tenuta Oliveto – Montalcino	Alberto, Aldemaro & Livia
Uccelliera – Montalcino	Andrea & Paola Cortonesi
Poggio Antico – Montalcino	Paola Glodder
Casanova Di Neri – Montalcino	Giacomo Neri & Family
Martn Del Nero – Resta	Anna Lisa Tempesti
Osteria Osticchio – Montalcino	
Fattoria del Cerro – Montepulciano	Giovanni Lai
Ristorante Calanova – Isola di Elba	
Osteria La Botte Gaia – Isola di Elba	Riccardo
Hotel Hermitage - Isola di Elba	
Tenuta dell'Ornellaia	Axel Heinz
Podere Sapaio	Massimo Piccin
Le Macchiole	Luca
Tenuta San Guido	Sebastiano, Elena & Nicolo'
La Pineta	Luciano Zazzeri
www.sailingtheweb.com	Marco
Hotel Dei Capitani	Montaleino
Gregg Hinlicky	Artist